Lois Duncan

KILLING MR. GRIFFIN

Edited by: Britt Keson
Illustrated by: Palle Schmidt

The vocabulary is based on
Michael West: A General Service List of
English Words, revised & enlarged edition, 1953
Birger Thorén: 10.000 Words for 10 Years of English, 1990
J.A. van Ek: The Threshold Level,
Council of Europe Press, 1990
The British National Corpus, Oxford, 1996

Series editors: Ulla Malmmose
and Charlotte Bistrup

Cover layout: Mette Plesner
Cover illustration: Palle Schmidt

Printed in Denmark by
Sangill Grafisk Produktion, Holme-Olstrup

Biography

Lois Duncan grew up in Sarasota, Florida. Ever since she was a young girl, she knew she wanted to be a writer, and she sold her first story to a magazine when she was thirteen. In 1962 she moved to Albuquerque, New Mexico, where she taught at the Journalism Department at the University of New Mexico while she continued to write for magazines.

Lois Duncan has written over 50 bestselling books for young people and adults, many of which have won awards. Some of her best-known novels are teenage suspense novels, which include: *Daughters of Eve, Don't Look Behind You, Down a Dark Hall, A Gift of Magic, I Know What You Did Last Summer* and *Killing Mr. Griffin*.

In 1981, Lois Duncan wrote a non-fiction book, *Who Killed My Daughter?*, about her search for the truth about the murder of her own 18-year-old daughter.

The phonetic transcription in the foodnotes follows British English pronunciation

Chapter 1

It was a very windy day when they got the idea of killing Mr. Griffin. As she walked to school in the morning, Susan McConnell had to hold on to her *glasses*. I hate this windy weather, Susan told herself. I wish I lived somewhere else. 5

"Get them!" someone shouted behind her. "Get them before they fly away."

Susan turned around to see David Ruggles running toward her. He ran past her, trying to catch some papers that were flying in front of him. 10

Susan put her foot down on one of the pieces of paper and picked it up. "Oh, it's dirty now!" she said. "I'm sorry."

"It doesn't matter." David took the paper from her hand. "The rest of it has blown away. One page is not 15 going to make any difference. If all of the pages aren't there, Mr. Griffin won't accept my homework. I've never done anything right for him yet."

"Neither have I. Neither has anybody, I guess."

Susan walked beside him to school. The wind was- 20 n't so bad after all, she thought. Now she, Susan McConnell, was walking beside David Ruggles, the most popular boy in school.

When they reached the door to the school building, Susan took off her glasses to clean them. She had 25 dreamed about David every night for the past year, but she had never dreamed about walking into English class together with him. Everyone, even Betsy Cline, would be watching them! Susan put her glasses on again,

| *glasses*, see picture, p. 6

glasses

but now David was walking ahead together with his friends, Mark Kinney and Jeff Garrett.

When Susan got to the door of the English classroom, David and his friends were already sitting at the back of the class, talking to Betsy Cline. She sat down next to 5 Betsy.

The bell rang and Mr. Griffin stepped into the classroom. Other teachers might be a little late, but never Mr. Griffin. He looked at them, and everyone stopped talking. 10

"Good morning, class," he said.

"Good morning, Mr. Griffin," they answered.

"Please take out your homework and pass it to the front."

Jeff raised his hand. 15

"Mr. Garrett?"

"I haven't finished mine yet. There was a basketball game last night, and I am on the team."

"Basketball isn't going to help you in my class," Mr. Griffin said. "Mr. Ruggles, your hand is raised. Do you 20 have something to tell me?"

"I did my homework, sir," David said, "but it blew away. I'll redo it tonight."

"I have never accepted late homework on windy days. Miss Cline?" 25

"I didn't understand what we were supposed to do," Betsy said, looking worried.

Susan read through her homework again. She usually got A's in all of her classes, but in English class she never got more than a B. 30

"Miss McConnell, are you finished?" Mr. Griffin asked.

7

"I'm sorry." Susan felt her face grow hot. "I was just checking my spelling."

"An excellent idea, but you should have done it sooner. Please hand in your homework now. Mr. Kinney, did you do your homework? No, I didn't think so. Those of you who have not handed in your homework, you will all *fail* this class. Now, open your books, please."

"But, Mr. Griffin, that's not fair!" Jeff said. "We should be allowed to try again."

"Why is that, Mr. Garrett?"

"Other teachers accept late papers!" Jeff said.

"What Jeff is saying, Mr. Griffin," Mark Kinney said quietly, "is that a lot of us really need to pass this class."

"Yes, we do!" Jeff said. "It's not fair to us, or to our parents, or to the school if you let us fail! Then we will all have to come back next year to take this class over again."

"That's an interesting thought, isn't it?" Mr. Griffin said. "Don't think that I won't fail you if I think your homework isn't good enough. I guess you will have to take my class again next year."

vial
[vaɪəl]

fail, not pass. If you fail a class, you usually have to take it over again

8

Mr. Griffin put his hand in his pocket and pulled out a small plastic *vial*. Then he took a pill from the vial and put it in his mouth.

"Please, open your books," he said.

From behind her, Susan heard Jeff Garrett say quietly, "That Griffin is the sort of person you'd like to kill."

Chapter 2

"Well, why don't we then?" Mark asked Jeff.

"Why don't we what?" Jeff said. They were sitting together with Betsy in the Snack-'n'-Soda Shop after school.

"Plan to kill him."

"Plan to kill him? You mean – *murder* – him?" Jeff put down his half-eaten hamburger. "You're *crazy*! You're *joking*, right?"

"You think so?" Mark asked.

"Well, aren't you?" Jeff wasn't quite sure. Sometimes he knew when Mark was joking, sometimes he didn't.

"Of course, he is," Betsy said and put her Coke glass down. "People don't go around killing the teachers they don't like. There wouldn't be any teachers left in the school."

"But it would help us," Mark said. "I've already failed his English class once. Well, I'm not taking it over again a third time. No way! You suggested something in class, Jeff. You said that you wanted to kill the man.

murder, commit the crime of killing (someone)
crazy, ['kreɪzɪ] not right in the head
joke, say something that is funny to make people laugh

9

Have you changed your mind?"

"What do you have in mind? And don't tell us you want us to murder Griffin. Betsy and I won't believe that."

5 "Griffin would, I think," Mark said quietly. "I think we should *scare* him. Nobody wants to get killed, not even Griffin."

"You mean we could write him a letter and *threaten* him?" Betsy asked.

10 "No," Mark said. "We don't want anything on paper. Besides, he wouldn't take it seriously. To show him that we mean business, we'd have to do it face to face."

"Go to his house and threaten him?"

"No. He's got a wife, doesn't he? We don't want any-
15 one else seeing it. No, here's my idea – we *kidnap* him. We take him up in the mountains someplace, and we show him what it's like to be scared."

There was a moment of silence. Then Betsy said, "I don't know. The idea is good, but kidnapping is a *crime*,
20 isn't it? The police would find us."

"Not if he doesn't know who we are," Mark said. "Not if we *blindfold* him, and he doesn't know who's got him."

"What if something happened?" Jeff said. "If he
25 found out that it was us?"

"It wouldn't be the end of the world. We're only

---

scare, make (someone) afraid, frighten
threaten, ['θretn] make (someone) afraid by saying one will hurt
30 him/her
kidnap, take (someone) by force and hold him/her against his/her will
crime, an action that is against the law
blindfold, ['blaɪnfəʊld] put something over someone's eyes so that he/she cannot see

10

children, aren't we? None of us is eighteen yet. We're just a group of fun-loving young people playing a joke. People do that sort of thing all the time. Look, if you are too scared, Jeff, just say so. There are plenty of others in that class who would help me. I can get all the help 5 I want without you."

"Well, I'm not scared," Betsy said quickly. "I think it's a great idea! I was just worried that we might get into some kind of trouble. But you're right, of course. Nobody would believe him if he told anyone. It would 10 sound too crazy."

"Jeff, are you with us?"

"I guess so," Jeff said slowly. "That does make sense. I mean, like Betsy said, people don't just kill their teachers. He'd sound crazy if he said anything. He'd 15 lose his job." He paused. "Are you getting anybody else into this?"

"A couple of others, maybe," Mark said. "There has to be someone to get Griffin into a place where we can get him. Someone he trusts. And there has to be some- 20 one to give us *alibis*. I suggest we ask Dave Ruggles."

"Dave wouldn't do something like this!" Jeff said.

"He'll do it," Mark said. "I'm sure of it. I've chosen Sue McConnell to help us as well."

"Sue McConnell?" Jeff said. "Who's that?" 25

"I know!" Betsy said. "It's that girl who is taking our English class. The quiet one with the glasses. Oh, Mark, you're just joking, of course. She would never do it!" She started to laugh.

"I'm not joking," Mark said. "I mean it. She's the 30 one."

---

alibi, ['ælɪbaɪ] something that shows that you were somewhere else at the time when a crime was committed

11

"Why her?"

"Well, she's an A-student, but Griffin has given her nothing but B's. Besides that, she has never been seen together with us before. Nobody would ever think we were planning this together with her."

"How do you think you're going to get her to be a part of this?" Jeff asked.

"Dave can do it for us," Mark said.

"Dave? How?"

"She's in love with Dave," Betsy said. "Mark's right about that. She sits in English class *staring* at him all the time."

"If Dave would put a little sunshine into her life," Mark said, "she'll do anything for him."

"What are you anyway, some kind of psychologist?" Jeff looked at his friend. "How do you know things like that?"

"I watch people. I notice things."

Jeff remembered the first time he had met Mark. Jeff had been twelve then, big for his age. His voice had already started to change. When he spoke, the rest of the class had laughed at him. He noticed that the new boy in class had been watching him. During lunch, the boy had come over to him and said, "You get angry too easily. That's not good."

"Who are you?" Jeff had asked angrily.

"My name is Mark Kinney. I'm new in town. I just moved here with my mother. I'm going to do something after school. Something really interesting. Do you want to come?"

---

stare, look at (something or someone) very long and hard

"What?" Jeff had asked, interested. "What are you going to do?"

"Do you like cats?"

"Not especially."

"Neither do I," Mark had said. "I've got a plan. Are you coming? I'll meet you behind the school at three-thirty."

"Okay, why not?" Jeff had said. He did not know why he had agreed.

Now, five years later, he heard himself saying again, "Okay, why not?"

"Good," Mark said and Betsy smiled.

"It'll be fun," she said. "Like a game. We ought to have something fun to remember from our time at high school."

"You'll tell your grandchildren about it," Mark said. "Griffin will be *begging* us not to kill him. That'll be something to remember, all right."

He wasn't smiling any longer. Mark didn't smile very often. Jeff remembered that he had noticed this the first day they had met – the day Mark had set fire to a cat behind the school.

Chapter 3

"Davy, is that you, dear?"

"Yes, Grandma," David Ruggles said. "Who else?"

"Aren't you going to come in to see me?"

---

beg, ask (someone to do something) with a lot of feeling

13

"Sure, just a moment." In the kitchen, David finished making his lunch and then went to his grandmother's bedroom. She was sitting in a chair by the window.

"Would you like me to make you some lunch?" he
5 asked her.

"Your mother went off to work this morning and forgot to make me lunch. I would really like some *Jell-O*."

"I'll make you some." David *sighed* and went back to the kitchen. He knew that his mother would never forget
10 to make lunch for his grandmother. He ate his lunch while he made the Jell-O for his grandmother. Then he went back into her room. "Do you need anything else?"

"Yes," the old woman said. "I have to go to the bathroom."

15 "Oh, Grandma, can't you wait awhile?"

"I've been waiting all day."

He knew this was not true, either. When his grandmother was alone in the house, she got up and did whatever it was she had to do. She just loved to tell
20 stories to get their attention. She had been living with David and his mother ever since her son, David's father, had left them. David really missed his father, whom he hadn't seen since he was a little boy.

"All right, Grandma," he said. "Okay. Hold on to me."
25 He helped her out of her chair and took her to the bathroom. "You okay now?"

"All right, Davy. I'll tell you when I want to go back."

"You do that. I'll be right here."

30 He sat down in the living room and stared at the

Jell-O, [ˈdʒeləʊ] popular American dessert made of gelatin
sigh, make a sound while you push air out of your lungs to show that you are either irritated, sad or tired

14

telephone. He thought of calling Mark, Jeff or Betsy. Most of the time they just drove around in Jeff's car. He knew he was welcome to join them. Mark had asked him more than once, and so had Jeff. David had said, "Thanks, but I've got things to do at home." He knew 5 they would never understand.

"Unless there is a reason," his mother had told him, "a really good reason, I want you to be at home in the afternoons. Your grandmother sits there alone all day, looking forward to you coming home from school." 10

The doorbell rang.

Who on earth? David thought and opened the front door.

Mark was standing there. "Jeff and Betsy are out in front in Jeff's car. Do you want to come for a drive? 15 We've got an idea we want to talk to you about."

"I can't right now. I've got things to do here." David thought of his grandmother in the bathroom. Any moment now she would be asking to be taken back to her room. "But I'll walk out to the car with you," he 20 said to Mark. "What did you want to talk about?"

"It will take too long to explain," Mark said. "The idea is this: we're going to *teach* Mr. Griffin *a lesson*."

"Teach him a lesson?"

"Scare him. Teach him that he can't do what he did 25 to us today."

"How are you going to do that?" David asked.

"We're going to kidnap him," Mark said. "We're going to make him think we're going to kill him."

"Oh boy," David said. "You could get into all kinds 30 of trouble."

teach someone a lesson, make (someone) feel sorry for what he/she has done

15

"I don't think so. Not if he is blindfolded. Not the way I'm planning it." Mark put a hand on David's shoulder. "How about it, Davy? Do you want to be a part of it?"

5 From behind him, David heard his grandmother's voice, "Davy?"

"Look," he said, "like I told you, I've got things to do. Later, I'll meet you at the Snack-'n'-Soda. Say around eight, okay?"

10 "No, it's not okay. I need to know **now**," Mark said. His hand was still on David's shoulder. "Dave, how long has it been since you did something crazy? How long has it been since you did something wild, just for fun?"

15 "You're not **really** planning to kill him?" David said slowly.

"No, just to scare him. Are you with us?"

David looked back at his house and thought about it. "Okay."

Chapter 4

20 The telephone woke Susan at nine-thirty on Saturday morning. Who can be calling so early, she thought. Why doesn't someone answer it?

"Sue!" her brother shouted. "It's for you."

"For me?" she shouted back. "Who is it?"

25 "How should I know? Some boy," her brother said. "Don't tell me you have a boyfriend!"

She got up and took the telephone from his hand. "Hello?"

"Hello, Sue?" a voice said. "This is David Ruggles."

16

It's a joke, Susan thought. "David who?" she asked, trying to make her voice sound normal.

"It's David Ruggles, from school. From your English class. The one whose papers you ran after yesterday, remember?" 5

"Oh, yes. Yes, of course. I know who you are." It was not a joke then. It was real. Or maybe she was still in bed, asleep and dreaming.

"It's such a nice day today," the voice on the telephone said, "and a group of us thought we'd have a picnic up in 10 the mountains. I was wondering if you might like to go."

"Yes," Susan said. "I'd love to go."

"You would? Great. We'll come by your house around eleven, then. Okay?"

"Okay," Susan said. "Okay, then, I'll see you in a little 15 while."

Susan put the telephone down and stood there. "I have a *date* with David!" she said to her brother.

At eleven o'clock the doorbell rang, and there he was.

"Have fun," her mother said, as Susan and David 20 walked to the car. David opened the door for her.

"You know everyone here, don't you?" he asked Susan. "This is Jeff, Mark and Betsy."

"Hello, Sue," Betsy said, smiling.

"Hi, Sue," Mark said, and Jeff said, "Great day for a 25 picnic, right? It's almost like summer."

They drove out of the city on the highway and along a long dirt road into the mountains. After a few miles, they stopped at the end of the road and got out of the car. 30

date, when a boy and a girl go out together, e.g. to eat dinner or see a movie

"This is the place," Mark said. "Lana and I used to come here all the time. You can't see it from here, but there's a *path* over there that leads to a *waterfall*."

"Who's Lana?" Susan asked David quietly while the others walked ahead.

"The girl Mark used to date, until Griffin stopped it. You've heard about that, haven't you? I thought everybody had."

"I haven't."

"Well, I'll tell you later," David said and smiled at her.

They heard the waterfall long before they saw it. The closer they got, the louder it became. Then, suddenly, it was right there in front of them.

"Wow!" Jeff said.

"I didn't know it was here!" Betsy said.

"Nobody does," Mark said. "Nobody ever comes here."

"It's simply beautiful!" Susan said. She felt that she should say something more, but she couldn't find the right words.

"Let's eat!" Jeff said.

They all sat down on a blanket and ate next to the waterfall. Afterwards, they lay on the grass and looked up into the sky. Susan took her glasses off.

"You look different without your glasses," David said. "Do you have to wear them?"

"Only if I want to see," Susan told him.

"I wonder what Mr. Griffin looks like without his glasses," Betsy said.

---

path, small way made by people walking (usually in a field or a forest)
waterfall, water falling down from a high place

Jeff started to laugh. "We'll have to take them off before we blindfold him."

"Blindfold him?" Susan said. She thought she had not heard correctly. "Did you say blindfold?" Suddenly, she realized that everyone was staring at her. 5

"You heard right," Jeff said slowly, and then they told her the things they were going to do. Later Susan could not remember exactly who told her what, but they all took turns telling her their plan.

"You're joking," Susan said when they finished. 10
"You're not really going to do it."

"Yes, we are," Jeff said.

"I don't believe you. It's like something out of a book. It's not real. You're making it up."

"You can help us if you want to," Betsy said. 15

"Me? How?" Susan asked.

"Mark will tell you. It's his plan."

"You can ask to see Griffin after school," Mark said. "Say that you want to talk to him about your home-work, or something. Keep talking to him until every- 20
one else has left the building. Then, when he walks out into the *parking lot*, we'll get him."

"You really think it would be that simple?"

"Sure. Why not?" Mark said. "The best things in life are simple. Simple things work. They don't go wrong." 25

"We all have our parts," Betsy said. "I will work out how to give everyone an alibi. The boys are going to blindfold Mr. Griffin so he won't be able to see who anyone is. Then afterwards he won't be able to tell any-one who did it." 30

"He'll know **me** if I talk to him after class," Susan said. "He won't be blindfolded then."

| *parking lot*, place where many cars are parked

"He won't even guess that you're part of it," Mark told her. "You'll leave before anything happens."

"I don't know," Susan said slowly. "I've never been mixed up in anything like this."

5 "Who has?" Jeff said. "It'll be the first time for all of us. My God, we've got to do something really wild just once in our lives. Let's have some fun while we can, and we'll teach Mr. Griffin a lesson at the same time."

"When would you want to do it?"

10 "What about Thursday?" Mark said. "That will give us time to get all the details worked out."

"Okay, Sue?" David asked.

"Well –" Susan said.

"Come on."

15 "Okay." She heard her voice speaking the word. Had she really said that? Had she really agreed to this?

"Good for you!" Jeff said, and Betsy laughed.

"I knew you'd join us, Sue!" she said. "That's what I told the others."

20 "That's my girl," David said softly and kissed her.

Never, Susan thought, never ever will I be as happy again as I am right now.

And she was right.

25

Chapter 5

The *alarm clock* rang at seven, and Kathy Griffin shut it off without opening her eyes. She reached for Brian in
30 the bed beside her, but he was already up.

That man, she thought. I don't know why he owns an alarm clock. He never uses it.

alarm clock, clock you use to help you wake up in the morning

20

A few moments later the bathroom door opened and Brian came into the bedroom.

"Good morning, Brian," she said and started to get up. "Should I make you some breakfast?"

He gave her a quick kiss as they went to the kitchen. 5

When Kathy first met her husband, three years ago, he had been an assistant professor in English at the University of Albuquerque. He had told her he wanted to teach English to high school students instead.

"Why?" Kathy had asked. 10

"Because many of the young people who go to university aren't good enough. You give them a book to read, and they can't tell you what it's about. It's too late to do anything about it at university."

"And what would you do as a high school teacher 15 that you don't do now?"

"I'd teach!" he had said. "I won't play games with them. I'd make sure that each one of them is doing the best work they can. I'd push them. By the time they finish my class, they will really be ready for university 20 work."

"You wouldn't be very popular, I'm afraid," she had said.

"I've never been very popular," he had answered.

Kathy Griffin finished making breakfast for herself and 25 her husband, and they sat down at the kitchen table.

"Could you call the *drugstore* and order some more pills for me?" he said. "I'll pick them up on my way home. That'll be a bit later than usual."

"Oh? A meeting?" 30

| *drugstore*, store that sells medicine (among other things)

21

"No, a student has asked to see me after class," he said. "She wants to talk about her homework. I'm meeting her at three."

"Is she one of your problem students?" Kathy asked.

5 "No, actually she's one of my good ones. Her name's Susan McConnell. She's a very good writer."

"Have you told her that?"

"Of course not. I don't want her thinking she's a *genius*. She still has things to learn." He stood up, ready
10 to leave.

"I think it's important that you let her know," Kathy said. "Have a good day, Brian. I'll phone the drugstore for you as soon as it opens. I love you. I'll see you tonight."

15 "Okay, see you later," he said and walked out the door.

Suddenly she thought, I don't want him to go. Something is wrong. Something *terrible*! I don't want him to go.

20 "Kathy!" he turned and shouted to her. "I love you."

"I know," she shouted back. "I know."

Chapter 6

At ten past three, David's grandmother was sitting in the chair by her bedroom window when she heard the front door open and close.

25 "Is that you, Davy?" she asked.

"Sure, Grandma, it's me."

He came into her room and bent down to kiss her.

genius, ['dʒiːnɪəs] very intelligent person
terrible, really bad

He put his books down on the table by her bed. "I've got something for you. A surprise. I'll be back in just a minute."

"A surprise? What in the world –"

A moment later he was back with a *bowl* in his hand. "Jell-O!" he said. "I made this especially for you before I left for school this morning."

"How nice, Davy," she said. "Aren't you going to have any?"

"Nope. I'm not hungry. I'll sit here, though, and watch TV with you while you eat it. How is it?"

"It *tastes* just fine," she said, taking a mouthful. "It's really good."

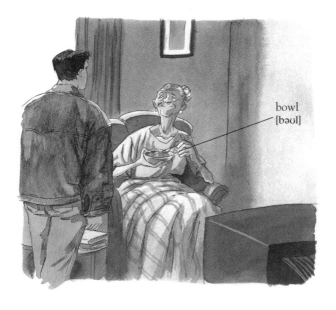

bowl
[bəʊl]

taste, experience (something, usually food) in one's mouth

23

Actually, it didn't taste as good as usual, but she didn't want to make him feel bad. She thought it tasted slightly *bitter*, but she continued eating.

When the bowl was empty, David carried it to the
5 kitchen and washed it carefully. His grandmother had her eyes closed when he got back.

"Are you tired, Grandma?" he asked.

"Of course not," she said without opening her eyes. "What should I be tired from? I'm not one of those old
10 people who need to sleep in the daytime."

He sat with her until she was asleep. Then he left the house and ran back to school.

Mrs. Cline was playing bridge at a friend's house when Betsy telephoned her.
15 "Hello, dear, is something the matter?" Mrs. Cline asked her daughter. She heard loud voices in the background. "Is that Jeff shouting?"

"Yes," Betsy answered. "He and Mark are here in my room listening to music right now. Jeff, be quiet! My
20 mother's on the phone, and I can hardly hear her!"

"Okay," Mrs. Cline said, "but don't play it too loud. Is that what you called about?"

"I just wondered if it was all right that they were here," Betsy said.
25 "Of course, but like I said, don't play your music too loud. The neighbors will hear it."

"Okay," Betsy said. "What time do you think you'll be home?"

"Oh, about six. Goodbye, dear." Mrs. Cline went
30 back to the bridge table.

At the Cline house, Betsy hung up the phone and

| *bitter*, with a certain kind of taste (not very pleasant)

24

turned off the *cassette recorder*. The music and shouting stopped. Then she turned up the radio before she left the house and drove to school in Jeff's car.

"I'm here now," David said, his face red, when he got to the school parking lot. 5

"Yeah, I see," said Mark coldly. "What took you so long?"

"I ran all the way from my house," David said. "The pills took much longer to work than I thought."

"You could have given her twice as much." 10

"I didn't know how strong they were. Too much could have killed her."

Mark looked at the door of the school building. "Get into the backseat of Griffin's car quickly, Dave. I think they're coming." 15

"They? You mean Sue is with him? She was supposed to leave before they got to the parking lot."

"That's what I told her, but now she's walking with him right out here." Mark turned to Jeff. "Dave is going to get him from behind. You know what to do? When 20 Griffin gets into the driver's side of his car, Dave will pull a bag over his head. As soon as he does that, you open the door on the other side and get into the car. Try to hold down his arms. I'll run around the front of the car and hold him from the driver's side." 25

"What about Sue?" Jeff asked.

"What about her? She'd better get out of the way, that's what. Are you ready?"

"As ready as I'll ever be," Jeff said. He wondered where Betsy was. She was supposed to be here with his 30

cassette recorder, [kə'set rɪˌkɔːdə] a machine for recording and playing music

25

car. Then he heard voices. Susan sounded nervous, but Mr. Griffin sounded normal.

"I didn't think my homework had to be perfect," Susan was saying.

5 "That's the whole point, Miss McConnell," Mr. Griffin answered. "Anything worth doing is worth doing perfectly."

They were beside the car now, on the side facing the building. Jeff and Mark were *kneeling* down on the other 10 side of the car, keeping their heads low.

"Thank you," Susan said, "for staying to talk to me."

"It's always nice to talk to a student who is serious about her work," Mr. Griffin said. He opened his car door and continued, "Have you far to go? I have to 15 make a brief stop at the drugstore, but I can drop you off at your house after that."

"Oh, no, no, sir, thank you anyway," Susan said, her voice high and nervous.

That idiot, Jeff thought angrily. In another minute, 20 she'll start crying.

Mr. Griffin got into his car and closed the door. Then he rolled down the window to say something to Susan. Jeff heard some noises and Mr. Griffin shouting.

"He's got him!" Mark shouted and they ran to the 25 car.

Jeff opened the car door and held down Mr. Griffin's arms. Mark opened the other door and started to tie the man's arms with a long piece of *rope*.

"Hold his arms!" Mark shouted.

30 "I'm trying!" Jeff shouted back.

| *kneel*, [niːl] have both knees on the ground

26

rope

Between the three of them, they managed to tie the rope around Mr. Griffin's body several times. Finally,

Mr. Griffin sat completely still.

"Okay, now I think we've got him where we want him," Mark said.

"What about the bag over his head?" David asked.
5 "He can't get much air in there."

"We've got to leave it on for now," Mark answered. "It keeps him quiet, and we don't want him shouting. When we get outside the city, we'll blindfold him instead."

10 "Do you think he can hear us with that bag over his head?"

"Not much, but don't use names or say something that you don't want him remembering later." Mark was smiling now. "Hey, didn't I tell you that we could do it?
15 It was just perfect!"

"So far, at least," Jeff said. "What'll we do now?"

"Just what we planned to do. Take him up to the waterfall."

"But my car isn't here yet," Jeff said.

20 "We'll take his. The girls can follow when the other car shows up. They know where to go."

From his place in the backseat of the car, David could see Susan standing several feet away. Her face was white and she had *tears* in her eyes.

25 "What's the matter?" David asked her.

"It was *awful*, just awful. You said you weren't going to hurt him."

"We didn't. He's fine."

"You said yourself that he can't *breathe*!"

---

tear, [tɪə] water that comes from the eyes
awful, really bad, terrible
breathe, [briːð] push air in and out of one's lungs
pass out, faint, lose consciousness

28

"If he *passes out*, we'll open up the bag. I'll watch out, don't worry. That's my job."

"We've got to go now," Mark said. "We don't have too much time if we want our alibis to work for us. You –" he pointed at Susan, "stay here and wait for ... the other girl. As soon as she gets here, you follow us. Got it?"

Susan's tears kept coming.

"Oh, Christ," Mark said. "Stop crying! Nothing's happened that wasn't supposed to happen. Do you know what you're supposed to do?"

"Yes," Susan said.

"Okay. We'll see you there."

Mark slowly drove Mr. Griffin's car out of the parking lot and into the street. Less than five minutes later, Jeff's car drove into the parking lot.

When Betsy saw Susan, she asked, "What happened? Where is everyone? Did everything go all right? Do they have him tied up and everything?"

"It went ... just like it was supposed to," Susan told her. "They said to tell you to meet them where we had the picnic."

"And I missed everything!" Betsy said. "Well, hurry up and get in the car." She looked at Susan's face. "Have you been crying? Did something go wrong?"

"No, nothing went wrong," Susan said. "I just don't want to go, that's all. I've done my part. What I said I would do. Now I don't want to do anything more."

"But this is the part we've all been waiting for!" Betsy's eyes were shining. "Sue, you don't want to miss this!"

"I said I'm not going."

"Well, it's your choice, I guess." Betsy started the car.

29

"I really don't understand you."

As Mark has said, it had all gone perfectly, just as they had planned it. But one thing happened that Susan did not expect. When the bag came down over his head, Mr. Griffin had shouted, "Run!" to her. He had been more worried about her than about himself.

Chapter 7

Betsy drove Jeff's car out to the end of the dirt road that led to the path to the waterfall. They might have waited, she thought angrily. They knew I was coming. They could have waited until I got there.

On her way out of the city, she had driven too fast and was given a *ticket* for *speeding*. The experience had been awful. "You may know my father," she had said to the policeman, "Harold Cline. He's a *County Commissioner*."

"I don't know any County Commissioners," the policeman had said, "and I'm glad. It makes doing my job easier."

Betsy parked her car next to Mr. Griffin's and walked down the path to the waterfall, where the boys were waiting for her. There on the ground before her, tied and blindfolded, lay Mr. Griffin. Mark and David were kneeling beside him.

ticket, (here) police statement that says you have done something wrong and are expected to pay money (a fine)
speeding, driving too fast
County Commissioner, important position in local (county) administration

"Where's Sue?" Jeff asked.

"She wouldn't come. She didn't want to. She looked like she'd been crying."

"That's all we need," Jeff said and put an arm around Betsy's shoulder. "I'm glad **you're** not scared."

"I wouldn't miss this for the world," Betsy said, watching Mr. Griffin's face.

"How do you like it being on the ground for a change?" Mark asked him. "It's not so great, is it, being down there where people can walk on you? Well, now you know how your students feel."

Mr. Griffin was silent.

"Well, how does it feel?" Mark said. "We want an answer. Did you hear me?"

"Yes, I heard you," Mr. Griffin answered. "If you know what is good for you, you'll untie this rope right away. If it's money you want, I don't have any on me."

"We don't want your money," David said.

"What do you want, then?" Mr. Griffin asked him. "Besides kidnapping me? If this is a joke, it's not funny. This is something I would expect from five-year-olds, not high school students. How many of you are there?"

"A lot," Jeff said. "Twenty! Twenty-five! Thirty!"

"That's *ridiculous*. There can't be more than three of you."

"There are lots of cars here," Jeff said. "None of us wanted to miss this."

"Miss what?" Mr. Griffin asked.

There was a short pause. Then Mark said, "Nobody wanted to miss watching you die."

"You want me to believe you brought me here to kill

ridiculous, [rɪˈdɪkjələs] very foolish, silly, not to be taken seriously

31

me? Just because you don't like the way I teach? That's ridiculous. How long are you going to keep playing this game? Take off the blindfold. I want to see who you are."

"How about begging us, Mr. Griffin?" Mark said quietly.

5 "Begging you?" Mr. Griffin asked. "To take off the blindfold?"

"We want to hear you beg," Mark said, his eyes shining. "We want to hear you begging us ... for your life."

"You really want me to believe you're planning to
10 murder me?"

"You'd better believe it, because it's true. Beg us, Mr. Griffin."

"I most certainly will not," Mr. Griffin said. "I don't believe you would do that. You have too much to lose."

15 "We don't have anything to lose. All we have to do is go home and leave you here. Nobody will ever find you. Nobody knows about this place but us."

"Look," Jeff said quietly to Mark. "Time's running out. We need to get back. Maybe we should untie the
20 ropes so he can get out of them and leave. What do you think?"

"I think you are crazy," Mark answered. "He doesn't get out of here until he begs. We agreed on that. You agreed too, didn't you, Jeff? He has to beg. Remember?"

25 "Well, yes, but it doesn't look like he's going to." Jeff looked worried.

"He's going to. Don't worry about that. He'll beg. Otherwise we'll leave him."

"Leave him?" Jeff asked. "You mean right here?"

30 "It's as good a place as any." Mark stood up. "Do you hear that, Mr. Griffin? You're in for a long, cold night. Want to change your mind?"

"Absolutely not."

32

"Your wife will worry about you," Mark said.

"I'm sure she will. She'll also call the police."

"A lot of good that will do her. They'll never look for you here, you can be sure of that." Mark looked at David. "Hey, what's with you?"

"Look," David said quietly. "We can't do that. It's carrying the game too far. Why don't we take him back now, the way we planned? He won't forget today, that's for sure. We've really scared him. That's what we wanted, wasn't it?"

"He hasn't begged yet," Mark said. "He's got to **beg**. Look, if we let him go now, he's **won**."

"Mark's right," Betsy said. "He called us 'five-year-olds.' He thinks we're ridiculous."

"Well, I don't like it," David said. "If we do leave him for a while, we'll have to come back up here later. We can't leave him here all night."

"Okay," Mark said. "We'll come back after Jeff's basketball game tonight. That'll give him plenty of time to think things over. To wonder if we're ever coming back. Are you with me?"

"Of course," Betsy said.

"It's not that long," Jeff said. "Until *midnight*. Maybe seven hours."

"Dave?" Mark said.

"I guess I don't have a choice, do I?" David said.

"That's right!" Mark walked past Mr. Griffin. "Goodnight, Mr. Griffin. Enjoy your own company. It's all you're going to have for a long time. Here's your last chance. Will you say, 'Please let me go.'?"

The man on the ground did not answer.

midnight, 12 o'clock at night

"Come on," Mark said. He led the way as the others followed behind him.

Chapter 8

The first time David called Susan that evening, Mr. McConnell answered the phone.

5   "I'm sorry," he said. "Sue's lying down. She doesn't feel too well tonight."

The second time he phoned her, an hour later, he got the same answer, this time from her brother. So he *borrowed* his mother's car and drove to Susan's house.

10   When David rang the doorbell, Mrs. McConnell opened the door.

"Oh, hello, David." She remembered his name. "Sue isn't feeling well, but I'm sure she'll want to see **you**. Sit down and I'll go and see if she's awake."

15   A few moments later she was back downstairs and her daughter was with her.

"Hello, David," Susan said quietly. She did not look him in the eye.

"I thought we could go somewhere and maybe get
20 something to eat."

"Why don't you, dear?" Mrs. McConnell said. "You hardly ate any dinner."

"Okay," Susan said. David could see that she did not really want to go.

25   They went out to the car and sat for a moment in silence.

Finally, David said, "Is the Snack-'n'-Soda all right?"

borrow, take (something that belongs to someone else) because one is allowed to

34

"Anyplace. I'm not hungry." Her voice was tired. "I couldn't eat anything right now if you paid me to. What did you do to him, Dave, after you left the school?"

"Just what we said we were going to do. We took him up to the place by the waterfall, and Mark tried to scare him. It didn't work very well."

"Was the bag still over his head?" Susan asked.

"No, of course not. We took that off as soon as we got out of the city. He's blindfolded."

"He **is** blindfolded?" Susan said, not believing what she had heard. "Do you mean he's **still** blindfolded? You didn't let him go?"

"Not yet," David said. "I thought we should, but the others didn't. Mark wants to hear him beg to be let go."

"You left him there!" Susan said.

"Don't be so *upset*," David said. "He's all right. Mark and Jeff are going back up there tonight after Jeff's basketball game. By then Griffin will say what Mark wants to hear. Then they'll bring him back to town and let him go, just like we planned. Don't worry, Sue. He'll be in class tomorrow, you'll see."

"I couldn't face him if he is," Susan said. "I'd start to cry if I even looked at his face. He thought –" She began to cry. "Didn't you hear him? He shouted, 'Run!' He wanted me to get away."

"You heard him wrong."

"David, I didn't!" Susan said. "He cared about me – he wanted to save me! We can't just leave him up there alone in the dark. It's too awful! We've got to go and get him!"

---

upset, very excited (not calm) because something bad has happened

"I told you," David said. "Mark and Jeff are going to do that. It won't be long now."

"How can you know that? It'll be very late, maybe midnight. Who knows – they might decide not to go at all. Maybe they'll tell each other, 'We'll do it in the morning.'"

"They wouldn't do that," David said, but even as he spoke he started to wonder. Was it possible that they would do exactly what Susan was suggesting? As she said, it would be very late, and Jeff would be tired and hungry after the basketball game.

"We've got to go up there right now," Susan said. "We can untie him and bring him down. It's gone too far, Dave. It isn't funny anymore. When you told me about it at first – at the picnic – I thought it would be … fun. But it isn't. It's … terrible."

David saw her tears. "Well," he said, "I guess we could do that. It's just that Mark would be so angry. When he plans something he likes it to go his way."

"Why should what Mark wants matter so much?" Susan asked. "We're in this just as much as he is, aren't we? Why shouldn't what **we** want matter?"

"You don't understand," David told her. "Mark isn't like other people. He's … he's …" He couldn't find the words. Mark was Mark. It was that simple.

"But Mark's not here right now, and we are. Please, David, we've got to go up there! We can't leave him there a minute longer!"

"Okay," David said and started the car.

They didn't talk much during the long drive to the mountains. They hadn't realized it would be so hard finding the dirt road in the dark.

"Is that it – that road there?" David asked. "That is a

36

road, isn't it? Yes, I think that's it."

"Let's try it," Susan said. Everything looked so different in the dark. "I can hardly see **anything**."

They drove on in silence until they got to the end of the road, where they parked next to Mr. Griffin's car and got out. The silence was all around them. It was the silence of the night.

"It's so – dark," Susan said.

"I'll get a *flashlight* from the car," David said. "Okay, are you ready?"

"Dave, think how dark – how terribly dark it must be – back where he is! Think how it must be for him lying there, all alone, not knowing if anybody's going to come – ever!"

flashlight

He took her hand. It felt small and cold in his. There was no reason for a girl like Susan to be here, he thought. Why did he bring her into this? he asked himself angrily. Why had he even gone along with it? It had been a *stupid* idea right from the beginning. People don't go around kidnapping other people just because they don't like them. "How long has it been since you did something crazy?" Mark had said. It was exactly what David had needed to hear.

When they reached the place where they had left Mr. Griffin, David stopped walking.

stupid, ['stju:pɪd] dumb, not intelligent

37

"He'll find out who we are, you know," he said quietly to Susan.

"I know," Susan said. "It doesn't matter. I mean, of course it matters, but we don't have any choice, do we?"

"I guess not," David said.

Mr. Griffin was lying exactly as he had been when they left him, straight and still, with the blindfold over his eyes. Susan ran over and knelt down beside him.

"Oh," she cried out. "Oh, Mr. Griffin, I'm sorry! I'm so sorry – so sorry –" She started to untie the rope. "David, help me get this off!"

"Here – his hands are tied behind his back," David said and knelt down beside her. "I'm sorry too, sir. This was a stupid thing to do. We'll untie your hands now."

The man on the ground did not move.

"He's asleep," Susan said, surprised. "How could he be asleep when the ground is so hard? Mr. Griffin, wake up! Please, wake up! We're here to take you home!"

"Move back, Sue," David said.

"But, we've got to wake him –"

"I said, move back. Let me take off the blindfold." He pulled the blindfold up over Mr. Griffin's head. Then he shone the flashlight straight into the man's face.

"His eyes are open," Susan said quietly. "He's not asleep. His eyes are open!"

"He's not asleep," David agreed.

"Then why doesn't he move? Why doesn't he say something? Mr. Griffin, it's Sue – Susan McConnell – from your English class, remember? Please, Mr. Griffin –"

David turned the light away from the man's face.

"He's not asleep," he said. "He's dead."

38

Chapter 9

We've got to get to Mark!

David kept thinking this over and over again.

We've got to get to Mark! Mark will know what to do.

He ran back down the path, pulling Susan behind him. Somehow, they found the car and got in. He drove down the dirt road and onto the highway.

We've got to get to Mark! Mark will know what to do. He said it aloud.

"To **do**? How can anybody **do** anything?" Susan said. "You can't make a dead person come alive." She wasn't crying anymore. "There's nothing that we can do," she said. "Now we're murderers."

"But we didn't kill him! We hardly touched him! It's true! He was fine when we left him."

"People don't just die, for no reason."

"Well, he did," David said. "We didn't hurt him. We only tied a rope around him. That could never kill anybody." He drove faster. "We've got to get to Mark. He'll know what to do – who to call."

"We could go to my house and get my dad," Susan said. "He'll help us."

"Mark first," David said. "We can't do anything until we tell Mark. My God, Sue, why did we have to be the ones to find him? If you hadn't said we should go up there it would have been Mark and Jeff. They'd have taken care of things. It was crazy for us to have gone up there without telling them!"

They drove to the high school parking lot. There were many people coming out of the school building, and many cars were leaving the parking lot. David ran inside and found Mark talking to Betsy while waiting for Jeff to change after the game.

"Is something the matter?" Mark asked when he saw him.

"He's dead," David said. The words flew out of his mouth.

There was a moment of silence. Then Mark said, "Griffin? How do you know?"

"Sue and I went up there. We looked at him. We're sure. He's dead, Mark."

"I believe you. Where's Sue? Why isn't she with you?"

"She's out in the car," David said.

"Get out there!" Mark said. "She might go to the police. Run! I'm going to wait for Jeff."

Betsy and David walked back out to the parking lot together.

"You didn't mean it, did you, David?" Betsy asked, looking scared. "It's all a joke, isn't it?"

"Yeah, a really funny joke," David said. What am I doing here? he thought. It's a dream, that's all. One of those dreams that seem so real, but you know that in a minute you'll wake up.

Mark and Jeff arrived, and everyone got into the car. For a moment, no one spoke. Then Mark said, "Well, Jeff, it looks like your dream came true. We really killed Mr. Griffin."

"We didn't!" Jeff said. "We hardly touched him!"

"Nobody will think we did," Mark said. "We've got our alibis, remember? David was with his grandmother all afternoon. You and I were at Betsy's house. And tonight most of us were at the basketball game. The best thing now is to show up at the Snack-'n'-Soda as usual and then go home."

40

"You mean – not tell anyone?" Susan said, surprised.

"Why should we do that?" Mark asked.

"Why, because – because – there's a man **dead**!"

"Would he be any less dead if we told people?" Mark asked. 5

"No, of course not. But you can't just have somebody die and not report it."

"If we reported it, we'd have to tell about the kidnapping," Jeff said nervously. "Who'd believe us when we explain how we were just having a little fun?" 10

"But it wasn't a real kidnapping," Betsy said. "It was a joke!"

"Who's going to believe that?" Mark said. "Betsy, your father is a County Commissioner. Just think what this would do to him. It would be in all the newspapers!" 15

"And my mother," David said. "There's no way I could tell my mother."

"We **have** to tell!" Susan said. "We don't have a choice! People will be looking for him! Mrs. Griffin will call the police. When Mr. Griffin doesn't show up to 20 teach tomorrow, everybody will know that he is missing."

shovel
['ʃʌvəl]

25

"Lots of people go missing – it happens every day," Mark said. "We will need to get rid of two things, the body and the car. Once those are gone there's nothing 30 left to worry about. It's too late to go up there tonight, and we have school tomorrow. It'll have to be tomorrow afternoon. Who can get hold of a *shovel*?"

41

"I can," Jeff said. "We have one at home. What will we do with his car?"

"We can park it at the airport," Mark said. "Cars get left there for months at a time. When they do find it, if they do, it will look like Griffin took a plane someplace."

"And – the body?" David asked. "You're planning for us to *bury* it?"

"That's simple enough. Right where it is now is a perfect place. Nobody ever goes there."

"No!" Susan cried. "We can't do that! Just put him in the ground! We can't say it never happened, that we're not responsible! We killed him, all five of us! Somehow we killed him!"

"I know how you feel," Mark said softly and put his arm around Susan's shoulder. "You and Dave found him, and that was very upsetting, but that's over now. You don't have to go up there again. The rest of us will take care of everything. It's going to be all right."

"It can't be all right," Susan said. "Mr. Griffin is dead!"

"Did you stop to think that he might be dead anyway?" Mark asked. "Only a sick person dies like that, without a reason. It could have happened anywhere – in his home, in school, walking down the street. Wouldn't it be awful if it had happened while he was driving his car and he drove right into a group of children waiting for the school bus?"

"If he had been at home his wife could have called a doctor," Susan said.

"My own dad was at home when he died," Mark said quietly. "It would have been better if he hadn't been.

bury, ['berɪ] put into the ground and cover with dirt

42

He was in his bed asleep when the house burned down."

"Oh, Mark!" Susan looked into his eyes. "How awful!"

"Yes, it was awful! The point is, when it's your time to die, you die. You can't change anything. If we went to the police, it wouldn't bring Mr. Griffin back, would it? It wouldn't help at all. Nobody needs to know, Sue. It's going to be all right. Just trust me, okay? It's going to be all right."

Susan cried while Mark held her. When she was done, he said, "Let's go to the Snack-'n'-Soda. We'll stay long enough to make sure that everyone sees us. Then we'll go home."

Chapter 10

"You're not eating much this morning," David's mother said at breakfast. "Are you upset about something, David? Did you and your friends have a fight last night?"

"No," David said. "We ate at the Snack-'n'-Soda late last night. That's why I'm not hungry now."

"Young people grow up so fast these days," his grandmother said. "I still can't believe that you are sixteen."

"I'm **seventeen**," David said.

"Oh, yes, dear. You told me that yesterday. Or was it yesterday? You start forgetting things when you get old. Yesterday was the day you went out with that boy Mark and stayed with him and his friends and didn't come home for dinner."

"It was **not**!" David shouted. "I came straight home from school yesterday. I got you some Jell-O, and you and I sat all afternoon and watched television. You do remember that, don't you, Grandma? **That** was yesterday."

"It was?" the old woman said. "One day is very much the same as the next when you're my age."

"You're not that old! You can remember," David said angrily. "Yesterday was Thursday, right? It was Wednesday when I went out with Mark and the others after school. Yesterday – Thursday – I came right home from school and gave you the Jell-O. Then we watched television all afternoon. I was with you in your room all afternoon!"

"David, for goodness sake," his mother said. "You don't have to shout at Grandma that way."

"I want her to remember!" David said.

"I remember, I remember," his grandmother said. "I remember the Jell-O you made for me. Where's the rest of it, Davy? Maybe you threw it out because it tasted strange?"

"Why would it taste strange?" David's mother asked. "Jell-O is Jell-O. It's all the same."

"It tasted great," David said. "That's why I ate all the rest of it. I just got started and couldn't stop, and I ate it all."

"You didn't eat any," his grandmother said. "I would have seen you eat it."

"You were asleep! You fell asleep almost as soon as I turned the TV on!"

"Goodness, I don't remember watching TV," his grandmother said with a laugh. "Did I really sleep? I never sleep in the daytime."

"I told you that I ate all the rest of it!" David shouted.

"Please, dear, don't shout!" his mother said. "I've

44

never seen you act like this, David. I've bought some more Jell-O for you, Grandma. David, you can make some more Jell-O for your grandmother, can't you?"

"Sure," David said. "I'll be happy to."

"That would be nice, dear." His grandmother smiled 5 at him. "And this time, Davy, be very careful what you put in it, won't you? The Jell-O you made last time was awfully bitter."

"I want to talk to Detective James Baca." 10

"Can you tell me what the problem is, Ma'am?" the young policeman at the front desk of the police station asked.

"My husband is missing," Kathy Griffin told him. "I phoned here last night and talked to somebody – I'm 15 not sure who – and he said to come in this morning and ask for Detective Baca."

"One moment, please." The young man showed Kathy to Detective Baca's office.

"Sit down, Mrs. Griffin," Detective Baca said as she 20 entered his office. "I heard about your call last night. Your husband still hasn't turned up?"

"No," Kathy said, sitting down. "There hasn't been a word. I'm so worried."

"How long has he been missing?" he asked. 25

"He didn't come home from work yesterday," Kathy told him. "I called the school this morning. They said that Brian was there for all his classes yesterday."

"So he's been missing since yesterday afternoon. Is that correct?" 30

"Yes. He was supposed to see one of his students after school. Susan – McConnell, I think her name is. And then – oh, I forgot to mention this, he was going to stop

45

at the drugstore to pick up some pills. He has a heart problem. It's painful, but he can control it. All he has to do is keep taking his pills, and then he's all right."

"Has he ever done anything like this before?" Detective Baca asked her.

"Never," she said. "Brian's always called me if he was going to be even a little late."

"Has he been worried about anything lately?"

"No more than usual. Brian's very serious about his teaching." She started to cry. "Something awful must have happened to him."

"There has to be an answer," Detective Baca said gently. "People don't *disappear* into thin air. Your husband is somewhere, and we'll do everything we can to find him. I'd like to talk to that student at the high school, the one who may have been the last person to see him yesterday."

Chapter 11

"Susan McConnell – come to the office, please!"

The words came through the *loudspeaker* over the classroom door. Susan felt her heart sink. It was the moment she had been expecting ever since she had arrived at school that morning.

loudspeaker

---

disappear, not be found anywhere, go missing

46

This can't be real, Susan thought. It's a dream, a *nightmare*. That's it – a nightmare. Soon I will wake up and I'll be back home in my bed. I'll open my eyes and see the sun shining through the window, and the birds will be singing in the trees outside.   5

But she had already woken up once that morning, and one could not wake up twice. Actually, she could not believe that she had slept at all. When she had gone to bed the night before, she had told herself, I will never sleep. When she got up in the morning and saw her   10
face in the bathroom mirror, she looked awful. I must have cried in my sleep, she thought. I must have cried all night.

When her mother saw her, she looked worried.

"You look just awful, Sue," she said. "Are you sure   15
you want to go to school?"

"I feel fine," Susan told her. She would have given anything at that moment to have said, "You're right, I can't go to school today," and gone back to bed. But the last thing Mark had said to them was, "You should all   20
show up for school tomorrow. We don't want to draw attention to ourselves. Okay?"

And when Mark told you something, you did it. She could understand now what David had meant when he had told her, "Mark isn't like other people." Now she   25
knew that if they did exactly what Mark told them to do, things would somehow work out. But it was important, terribly important, to do exactly as Mark said.

So she had gone to school and was sitting in class when she was called to the school office. Everyone turned to   30

| *nightmare*, bad dream

47

stare at her as she got up and left the classroom.

Mark was standing outside in the hallway.

"What are you doing here?" Susan asked him.

"Waiting for you," he said.

5 "How did you know –"

"I was watching the parking lot. I knew that when the police got the report that Mr. Griffin was missing, they'd send a car over here to the school. This is the last place he was seen, and you're the last person to

10 have seen him."

"I'm scared," Susan said. "I don't know what to tell them. If they've found out everything –"

"They haven't found out anything," Mark said. "All they know is that Mr. Griffin didn't go home last night

15 and didn't come to work this morning. That's all. Nothing else. The only way they're going to find out anything else is if you tell them."

"They'll ask me questions –"

"And you'll give them answers," Mark said. "You

20 wanted to meet Mr. Griffin to talk about your homework. Tell me what happened after you met him."

"We talked about my homework, and I had to walk out to the parking lot with him. I hadn't meant to, but I couldn't just say 'Goodbye' and walk away from him

25 while he was talking."

"So you walked with him out to the parking lot, and then what?" he asked.

"He asked if he could give me a ride home."

"No, he didn't."

30 "He – didn't?" Susan asked.

"No," Mark said. "He had other plans. Say that while you were talking to him, he was acting very strangely. He kept looking at his watch. His mind was

48

on something else."

"But, that's not true," Susan said.

"Sure, it's true. That's how a man acts when he has a woman on his mind."

"I don't understand." 5

"When you walked out of the parking lot, you looked back. You saw him getting into his car, and there was a woman in it. A young and beautiful woman."

"But, there wasn't!" Susan said. "I can't say a thing 10 like that!"

"Of course, you can," Mark said. "You can say anything you want to. You're the last person who saw him, aren't you? Who else is going to know who was in that car? You're the one who saw him get into it and drive 15 away."

"But why?" Susan asked. "Why make up something like that? What good will it do?"

"It'll stop them from looking at us. Right now they probably think his students had something to do with 20 this. When they start asking questions about his students, they'll find out who had problems with him, and that's us. So what do we do? We tell them about this woman, and they'll start wondering about her. Who is she? Where did she come from? Why did they drive off 25 together?"

"I can't do that, Mark," Susan said. "Mr. Griffin was married, you know. How would his wife feel, hearing something like that? She'd think —"

"She'd think that he had left her. What's so bad 30 about that? If she really loved him — and it's hard to believe that anyone would — then wouldn't she rather think that he was having a good time someplace than that he was dead?"

"Well – when you put it like that –" Susan said.

"You'd better get down to the office now," Mark said quickly. "They're waiting for you."

5 "Mark, come with me! I'm scared."

"You can do it," Mark said. "Everyone will believe you."

"I'll try," Susan said. "And after school?"

"You just go home like you would on any other day.
10 The rest of us will go up to the mountains and move the car and whatever. Okay?"

"Okay," Susan said. "If you say so, Mark."

She walked down the hall to the office door and went inside.

15 "Christ," Mark said to himself and sighed.

Chapter 12

At three-thirty Mark, David, Jeff and Betsy got into Jeff's car and drove into the mountains. The afternoon was warm and still.

"It's like last Saturday all over again," Jeff said and
20 laughed. "We're even sitting in the same places in the car."

"I wish it **were** last Saturday," David said and sighed.

"Okay, now," Mark said, "we're almost there. There's his car. Stop here next to it and let's get going. We
25 don't have a lot of time. Get the shovel."

When they reached the waterfall, Betsy cried out and covered her face with her hands. "Oh, God – there are **flies** on him!"

"What did you expect?" Mark said, laughing. "He

50

doesn't know the difference."

"Ugh!" Betsy said. "I've never seen a dead person before except at a *funeral*."

"This **is** a sort of funeral," Mark said. "Let's bury him there beside the water. Jeff, you're strong. Why don't 5 you starting digging? Dave, you help me move the body. We don't have to bury his *wallet* with him, if it's full of money."

"Is that it, there in his pocket?" David asked.

"Yes, here it is," Mark said. "There are only a few 10 dollars and some credit cards here. Hey! That gives me an idea! Once, when I was younger, I borrowed my father's credit card. I spent his money for a whole month before he discovered what I had done. I could borrow Mr. Griffin's credit cards. Wouldn't that be 15 fun?"

"You're a genius," Jeff said as he dug. "Dave, will you take over?"

David and Jeff took turns digging while Mark stood watching them with his hands in his pockets. 20

"That should do it," he said after a while. "It would be better if we dug deeper, but there just isn't time for that. Let's put the body in the hole. Dave, what are you doing?"

David had taken off his jacket and laid it over the 25 face of the man on the ground.

"Just – just –" David was kneeling beside the dead man. "I thought – his eyes – ought to be closed. And my jacket will keep the dirt off him."

"He won't know the difference." 30

"**I** will, though," David said. "I don't want the dirt to

---

funeral,['fju:nərəl] ceremony when a dead person is buried
wallet, something in which a man keeps his money

4*   51

be right on his face."

"It's your jacket. Are we ready? Jeff, take his shoulders. Dave, get his feet."

They lifted up the body, put it in the hole and covered
5   it with dirt.

We should have said a *prayer*, David thought. "He doesn't know the difference," Mark had said, and he was right, of course. David watched Mark, who was laughing and talking loudly with Jeff. Who is this person?
10 David asked himself. It was as though all the life that had left Mr. Griffin had gone right into Mark Kinney.

"Well, it's over and done now, and all that's left is the car," Mark said. "Betsy, you drive Griffin's car down to the airport. Don't worry, nobody will notice you.
15 Dave, you go along with her. Leave the car unlocked and the key in the car."

"Why should they leave the key?" Jeff asked. "Somebody might *steal* it."

"That's the whole idea," Mark said, laughing. "Can
20 you think of a better way to get rid of a car than to have somebody steal it?"

"You've really thought of everything," Jeff said.

"What if I get stopped?" Betsy asked. "The police will be looking for the car."

25 "Just drive slowly and carefully," Mark said. "Dave will be looking for police cars. If you see a police car, just park in front of a house as if you live there, and it'll drive right past you."

"All right," Betsy said nervously.

---

prayer, [preə] words you say to God
steal, take (something that belongs someone else) without being allowed to

52

David and Betsy didn't have much to say to each other as they drove into town. As Mark had said, nobody paid any attention to them. They reached the airport without any problems and pulled into the parking lot.

"Where should I park? Does it matter?" Betsy asked. 5

"I can't think why. Anywhere will do." Suddenly David looked back. "Oh no, there's a police car behind us."

"Right here in the parking lot!" Betsy looked in the mirror. "He followed us – or did he? Maybe he's just 10 parking here. What shall I do?"

"You don't have a choice," David said. "Just park somewhere. If you turn around and drive out again, he will notice us for sure."

"I'll park here," Betsy said. "Is he still behind us?" 15

"No, he's driven past us. I think you're right, he's going to park."

"Oh, thank heaven!" Betsy said and opened her door. "Let's get out of here!"

They got out of the car and saw that the police car 20 was parked nearby. The policeman was standing next to it.

"We'll have to walk right by him," Betsy said.

"That's okay," David told her. "If he had recognized the car as Mr. Griffin's car, he'd have done something 25 by now." He took her arm. "Walk slowly, keep your eyes on my face, keep talking, and remember to smile! He won't even notice us."

Betsy smiled brightly as they walked by. "It was just such a great basketball game last night!" she said to 30 David. "Jeff got the ball and –"

"Good afternoon, Miss Cline," the policeman said as they passed him.

Chapter 13

The story was on the six o'clock news, and Mr. McConnell mentioned it at dinner.

"On television this evening they were telling about a teacher who's been reported missing," he said.

"Missing?" Mrs. McConnell said. "Do you mean he simply disappeared?" 5

"That's right. He taught his class and then was never seen again. His name's Brian Griffin. Sue, don't you have a class with him?"

"Yes," Susan said quietly, "English." 10

"I wish my teachers would disappear," Susan's brother said.

"Don't joke about something like this," his mother said. "Personally, I can't think of anything more awful to happen." 15

I am not going to think about him, Susan told herself. I will make my mind think of other things. I am not Susan any longer, she thought. I am not the person my family know as their daughter and sister. I am a stranger who has done things they could not even imagine. 20 They look at me and call me "Sue," and when I speak back to them, they can never guess how far away from them I am.

The doorbell rang as they were clearing the table after dinner. 25

"You might as well get it, Sue," her mother said. "It will probably be David."

But it was not David who stood at the door when Susan went to open it. It was a woman in a brown jacket. 30

"I'm looking for Susan McConnell," she said. "I'm Mrs. Griffin."

For a moment, Susan could not move. She just stood there, staring at the woman's face.

5 "Who is it, Sue?" her mother called from the kitchen. When Susan did not answer, Mrs. McConnell came into the hallway.

"I'm Mrs. Griffin," the woman said again. "Kathy Griffin. I'd like to talk with Susan."

10 "Mrs. Griffin? The wife of Sue's teacher?" Mrs. McConnell came quickly over to her. "Please come in, Mrs. Griffin. We just heard the news about your husband and are so worried. Is there anything new since the report on the evening news?"

15 "No, nothing," the woman said and came inside.

"Come, sit down," Susan's mother said. "Can I get you some coffee?"

"No, thank you." Mrs. Griffin looked very tired. "I just want to talk to your daughter for a few minutes.
20 According to the police, she was the last person to see my husband yesterday, and she told them some things that I just can't accept."

"Sue was the last person to see him?" Mrs. McConnell turned to Susan in surprise. "You didn't tell
25 us that."

"Didn't I?" Susan said. "I thought I did."

"Of course you didn't," her mother said. "Ed, come out here, dear. Mr. Griffin's wife is here to talk with Sue."

30 I cannot go through with this, Susan thought, and yet there she was, sitting on the sofa between her parents, across from Mrs. Griffin. She heard herself say, "Yes, I |met him after school."

fireplace

"He told me about your homework at breakfast," Mrs. Griffin said. "He said it was very good. I know Brian isn't an easy teacher," she explained to Mr. and Mrs. McConnell. "He pushes his students very hard. Too hard, I sometimes think. He wants to bring them as far as possible before they leave high school. He considers Susan one of his 'good students'."

"That's very nice," Mr. McConnell said. "I'm sure it must mean a lot to Sue to hear that."

"It's because of that – because she is special to him – that I couldn't believe –" Kathy Griffin looked directly at Susan. "Why did you *lie* to the police about what Brian did when he left school?"

There was a moment of silence.

Then Susan said, "I don't know what you mean."

"Of course you know. You lied about several things at the interview. You told the police that Brian was nervous, that he kept looking at his watch and wasn't listening to what you were saying. I know that's not true. Brian was always very serious when talking to students about their work. He cared very much about them and would not have done what you said."

"He did," Susan said. "Mr. Griffin kept looking at his watch."

"What would you say if I told you Brian wasn't wearing a watch?"

"He was," Susan said. "He always wore a watch." She paused. "Didn't he?"

"Usually, yes," Mrs. Griffin said. "But the day before yesterday it broke. Right now, it's at home on his desk."

Oh, dear God, Susan thought. "Maybe he borrowed a watch from somebody, just for the day?"

| *lie*, not tell the truth

"Why would he do that? There are clocks all over the school. Every classroom has one. Why did you lie about the watch, Susan?"

"I didn't," Susan said. "I thought he was wearing one. He acted as though he were. He kept – he kept looking down at his *wrist* – the way somebody does who is used to wearing a watch. Maybe he forgot that it was broken."

"That sounds *reasonable*," Mr. McConnell said quietly. "What I'd like to know, Mrs. Griffin, is why is it so important if your husband was or wasn't wearing a watch?"

"It's important if it means that Susan isn't telling the truth. Susan, why did you say there was a woman waiting for Brian in his car?"

"Because there was."

"No, there wasn't. That's another lie!" Kathy said. "You lied. Why?"

"I didn't lie," Susan said. "There was a woman. Young, very pretty."

"What was she wearing?"

"A green jacket," Susan said quickly. "And a green sweater. And pants – brown pants."

"You could see her pants even though she was sitting inside a car?" Kathy asked.

"When Mr. Griffin opened the door to get in, I could see her pants."

"On your way across the parking lot, you looked back over your shoulder and you could see what color pants the woman in the car was wearing?"

wrist, [rɪst] what connects your hand to the rest of your arm. You wear your watch on your wrist
reasonable, believable, likely

59

"Mrs. Griffin," Susan's father said, "if Sue says she saw this woman, then she saw her. There's no reason for her to tell you this if it isn't true."

"That's the whole point," Kathy Griffin said. "There **must** be a reason. There has to be a reason for Susan to have told the police all these lies."

"That's ridiculous," Mrs. McConnell said. "Susan does not lie. She's our daughter! We **know** she doesn't lie."

"I feel exactly the same way about my husband," Kathy Griffin said. "I **know** him, and I **know** he did **not** leave the school with another woman. Something else happened to Brian, something I can't even begin to imagine, but Susan can. Susan knows what it is, or she wouldn't being lying to us."

"Are you saying that our daughter did something to your husband?" Mr. McConnell asked.

"Not by herself. Or maybe not at all. Maybe she just knows something about someone else who did. Maybe she **saw** something."

"Did you see something, Sue?" her father asked.

"No, of course not! I didn't see anything that I haven't already told you about!" Susan shouted. "I saw a woman in Mr. Griffin's car. I didn't see anything else or anyone else – just that."

"If our daughter says –" Mr. McConnell began.

The doorbell rang. Susan's brother opened it and came back with David and Mark.

"This is David Ruggles, a friend of Sue's," Mrs. McConnell said. "And I see you have another friend with you."

"This is Mark Kinney," David said.

Thank God! Susan could have thrown her arms

around both of them for coming. They both shook hands with Mrs. Griffin.

"I'm sorry," David said. "I didn't know you had company. Mark and I were wondering if Sue would like to get a Coke or something." 5

"I'd love to," Susan said and stood up. Anywhere, anything, to leave this room.

"Mrs. Griffin may have more things to ask you, dear," Mrs. McConnell said.

"I don't have anything else," Kathy Griffin said 10 quietly. "Are you boys in my husband's class also?"

"Yes," David said.

"What was your name – Ruggles? Yes, of course, Brian mentioned you. Your paper blew away on your way to class. Is that right?" 15

"Yes," David said again, surprised. "He told you about it?"

"Brian talks a lot about his students. And, you –" she turned to Mark, "are Mark Kinney. There was something last year – oh, I remember. You're the boy who 20 copied a paper from the university. You had to take Brian's English class over again this year."

"I'm afraid so, Mrs. Griffin," Mark said, looking down at the floor. "I was going through some problems and I made some mistakes." 25

"There was a girl who got the paper for you. She was a university student, right?"

"I guess she must have been," Mark said.

"Her name –"

"I don't remember her name anymore. Like I said, it 30 was a bad time for me."

"I'm sure I'll remember her name if I think about it," Kathy Griffin said and stood up.

61

Susan's parents stood up as well. "I'm sorry Susan couldn't be of more help to you, Mrs. Griffin. I know how upset and worried you must be. If we can help you in any way –"

5   "Thank you," Kathy Griffin's eyes were not on Mrs. McConnell, but on Susan. "I think Susan can be of more help, if she wants to be. Maybe she will remember something later and will contact me."

"If she does, I'm sure she'll call you at once," Mr.
10 McConnell said. "Won't you, Sue?"

"Of course," Susan said.

Chapter 14

"Davy's *been up to something*," David's grandmother said to his mother. "He's meeting his father, and he doesn't want us to know about it."

15   "His **father**?" David's mother said in surprise. "His father? His father left us many years ago! David hasn't been seeing his father. What is it with you and David these days?"

"No, I really mean it. Davy's been up to something.
20 The day he made Jell-O –"

"David was with you all Thursday afternoon," his mother said with a sigh. "It's not his fault that you fell asleep and don't remember."

"He wasn't here. He went out. And I think he met
25 his father. I've got *proof*. Real proof." She put her hand into her pocket and smiled. "I've got proof."

be up to something, plan to do something, often without telling anyone
proof, something that shows beyond a doubt what has happened

Detective Baca held the plastic vial carefully in his hand and read the name on it.

"Now, where exactly did you say you found this?" he asked.

"Up in the mountains at a place I like to go to some- times," the girl told him. "My former boyfriend and I used to go up there to have a picnic."

"You know Brian Griffin personally?" Jim Baca asked the girl.

"Well, not exactly. My boyfriend took his English class last year and had some – problems. I was – sort of – mixed up in it, and I remembered the name. Then last night I saw on TV that he was missing."

"Why were you so surprised to find this where you did?" the detective asked.

"It's not a public picnic place. I didn't think that anyone else knew about it. I guess, maybe, it was stupid, bringing it down to the police station."

"It wasn't stupid at all," Jim Baca told her. "It may be very important. Now, what about the rest of the area? Was there anything else lying around? Maybe some- thing that looked like someone had had a picnic up there?"

"No," the girl said. "But there was something strange. The ground looked like someone had been digging there."

"Well, it's about time you got here," Mark said angrily to Betsy when she arrived at the Snack-'n'-Soda to meet the others. "Where's Jeff?"

"He'll be late," Betsy said, sitting down across from him. "He's playing basketball. You said if we didn't continue doing the things we usually did, people would start wondering."

"Betsy, you've already started them wondering."

"What do you mean?" Susan asked quietly. "What has Betsy done?"

"She got a speeding ticket," Mark said.

"What's so awful about that?" Betsy asked. "Lots of people get tickets."

"How could you be at home listening to music with Jeff and me, when you're getting a speeding ticket at the same time?" Mark asked.

"Mark, it was just such a little thing that I never even thought about it until now."

"How much did you talk to the policeman?" Mark asked.

"Not much. I told him that my father is a County Commissioner."

"Well, no wonder that he remembered you," Mark said angrily, "when he saw you again in the airport parking lot, getting out of Griffin's car."

"What can we do?" asked David. "Go down and move the car?"

"We'll have to. There's no time to sit and wait for it to be stolen. But where can we put it?"

Just then, Jeff came into the Snack-'n'-Soda and sat down next to them. His face looked strange.

"What happened?" Mark asked.

"I heard it on the car radio," Jeff said. "They've found it."

"Then we don't have to worry about moving it from the airport parking lot anymore," Betsy said. "What did they say, Jeff? Did they say anything about Dave and me being seen in the parking lot?"

"They didn't find the car," Jeff said quietly. "It's the body. They've found Mr. Griffin."

"That's impossible," Mark said. "It's some kind of trick. Nobody knows that place but us. There's no way they could have found him already."

"They say they did. His wife has identified him. They said his wallet was missing."

"I knew it," Susan said. "There's no way we could have gotten away with it."

"It's a trick. They're just guessing that his wallet would have been stolen," Mark said. "Did they mention Dave's jacket?"

"No," Jeff said. "They said the wallet was gone, and his university ring was missing from his finger."

"Well, that *proves* it's a trick," Mark said. "We didn't take any ring. They're just trying to scare us."

"Do you still want to move the car?" Betsy asked.

"Yes, the sooner the better. David, can you go with Betsy and move the car?"

"Sorry," David said. "I promised my mother I'd be home at five o'clock. I'll drive Sue home first, though."

"Well, Jeff can go with Betsy, then," Mark said. "I'm going to get rid of Mr. Griffin's wallet and credit cards."

"If you don't think they've really found him," Susan asked quietly, "then why are you getting rid of everything?"

Mark did not seem to hear her. He got up and left the table.

30

prove, show (that something has happened beyond a doubt)

Chapter 15

"Where are we going?" Susan asked. "This isn't the way to my house."

"We're driving to my house first," David told her. "There's something I've got to get there."

"You're going to report it, aren't you?" Susan said suddenly.

"Report it? You've got to be joking."

"Joking? About **that**?" She put her hand on his arm. "We could drive down to the police station and – just tell them. We could explain how it all happened – how we never meant it –"

"Don't talk that way," David said. "Don't start thinking like that. It's too late. They'd never believe us. We've waited too long. Maybe you were right in the first place when you wanted to go to your father. But now it's too late. Mark is even getting rid of the credit cards."

"Mark says it's a trick – that they didn't really find him. They said a ring was missing."

"It isn't a trick," David said quietly. "The part about the ring is right. It wasn't on his finger because I took it."

"You – what?" Susan couldn't believe she was hearing him correctly. "You took off his ring – and kept it? How could you do such a thing? Why?"

"I don't know. I've asked myself that question a hundred times. I just know that when I saw that ring on his hand, there was something about it that made me feel –"

"Feel, how?" Susan asked.

"As though – it were – mine," David said slowly. "It

66

was as though it were something that belonged to me a long time ago, and I had lost it."

"That doesn't make sense," Susan said. "We can't keep *secrets* from Mark. Mark has to know everything, or he won't be able to tell us what to do."

"If Mark knew about the ring, all he'd do would be to tell me to get rid of it fast. That's why we're going to my house. I'll get it and throw it away somewhere on the way over to your house."

When they opened the door to David's house, his grandmother shouted, "Davy, is that you?"

"Sure, Grandma, it's me," he shouted back. He took Susan to his bedroom and started looking for the ring.

"Grandma," he said after searching for a while, "has anybody been in my room today? I can't find something I put here yesterday."

"Things get lost sometimes," David's grandmother said. "Especially little things."

"Grandma, have you taken something from my room?"

"Now, why would I do that?" the old woman asked. "Maybe your father came and took it?"

"My **father**? What do you mean by that?"

"Now, don't play games with me, Davy," his grandmother said. "I know my son's university ring when I see it."

"What have you done with the ring?"

"It wasn't yours, Davy," she said. "It was your father's. Your father was wearing that ring the day he left this house. The only way you could have it is if he's

---
| *secret*, ['siːkrət] something that only very few people know about

come back again and has given it to you."

"Grandma, that is not my father's ring," David said. "I haven't seen my father since I was a little boy. You've got things all mixed up."

5 "I'm an old woman, Davy, and I want to see my son before I die."

Susan closed her eyes. When I open them again, she told herself, this room will disappear. Ten years will have gone by, and I will be far away from here. I will
10 think back and ask myself, where was I ten years ago? What was I doing? What was I feeling? And I won't even remember. But when she opened her eyes once more the room was still there.

"Come on, Sue," David said in a low voice, "I'll walk
15 you home."

"But you haven't gotten what we came for!" Susan said.

"That's okay, I'll get it later. Grandma will change her mind."

20 No, she won't, Susan thought. She will keep that ring until David's father shows up. And then, if he doesn't show up, she'll show the ring to David's mother.

"You don't need to walk me," she said to David. "It's not that far. I can go home by myself." Susan turned
25 away from him and shouted to his grandmother, "I'm glad to have met you, Mrs. Ruggles."

Then she rushed out the door and ran to her house. We've got to do something, but what? Susan asked herself. David could not take care of the situation alone.

30 There was one person who would know what to do. One person who always knew what to do.

Susan walked in through the front door and went straight to the telephone.

68

"Hello, is this Mrs. Garrett?" Susan said. "I'm trying to get in touch with Mark Kinney. Is he there with Jeff? Oh, good. Please, can I speak to him?"

Chapter 16

The Sunday newspaper carried the complete story.

"Terrible," Mr. McConnell said. "Unbelievable. What kind of person would do such a thing! All that was missing when they found him were a couple of dollars, his credit cards and his university ring."

"His poor wife!" Mrs. McConnell said. "How awful this is for her! It says here that the funeral will be on Tuesday. You will be going to it, won't you, Sue?"

"No," Susan said. "Mother, I just can't."

Susan could not take her eyes off the photograph of Mr. Griffin's face on the front page. Susan had looked into those eyes every morning during the past school year.

Good morning, class.

Good morning, Mr. Griffin.

"Sue, dear," her mother said. "I know how you feel and how hard it must be for you, but you really ought to go."

"Does it say how he was killed?" Susan's brother asked.

"There were no signs on the body," Mr. McConnell said. "He had a history of heart problems, though. It says here that the police discovered the body after talking to a girl named Lana Turnboldt. She and a former boyfriend used to have picnics in the area."

"We ought to send flowers," Mrs. McConnell said.

69

Kathy Griffin lay on her back in bed, staring up at the *ceiling*. Without thinking, she turned and reached into the bed beside her. It was empty.

Somewhere in the house the telephone rang. It rang only once. A moment later the bedroom door opened.

"Oh – you're awake," a woman's voice said.

"Yes," Kathy said.

"What can I get you? Coffee?"

"I don't know. Yes, coffee, I guess. You haven't been here all night, have you, Rose?"

"Of course I have. What else are neighbors for?" the woman said. "There have been a lot of phone calls already. I've written down all the names."

"That's good of you, Rose," Kathy said and sat up. "How do they know about it already? Is it in the newspaper?"

"It's on the front page," Rose said. "You don't want to read it all, though. It'll only upset you."

"Reading about it isn't going to make it any worse. Maybe when I read it, it will start to make sense. Who could possibly hate Brian enough to do such a thing?"

"They'll find him. That's what the police are for."

"But they don't know where to start," Kathy said. "When I was with them yesterday, I couldn't think straight. There was something – the name of somebody – that meant something to me. I remember recognizing the name. I started to tell them, and then I couldn't remember any longer what I was going to say because I was so upset."

The telephone rang again.

"I'll get that," Rose said, "and I'll bring you coffee."

ceiling, ['si:lɪŋ] the top part of a room, above the walls

70

"And the newspaper," Kathy said.

At eleven-thirty on Sunday morning, David's grand-mother sat in her chair by the window, playing with the ring.

She had begun to realize that the university ring did not belong to her son after all. "I haven't seen my father since I was a little boy," David had said to her, and when he said it, she knew it was true.

"Grandma, please let me have it," he said to her just before he and his mother had left for church that morning.

"Have what?" she had asked him.

"You know," he had said in a low voice so his mother wouldn't hear. "It's really important to me. You don't know how important it is. Where is it?"

"David, aren't you ready yet?" his mother had shouted from the living room.

And so he had left with a worried look on his face. David had been very upset, as upset as she had ever seen him.

There is something very wrong here, she thought. Where had this ring come from, and why was it so important? She turned the ring slowly in her hand. Could David have stolen the ring? She didn't think so.

Lost in her thoughts, David's grandmother did not hear the front door open. When she heard it close again, she thought, could time have passed so quickly? Were David and his mother back from church already?

"Davy," she called, "is that you?"

There was no answer.

"Davy?" she said again, looking at her bedroom door. Then she lifted her hands to her face, and the ring fell

71

to the floor.

"Why, you're not Davy!" she said to the boy who had come into her room.

Chapter 17

The wind began to blow again early Sunday afternoon. Susan's family had gone to a church dinner, and she was beginning to wonder if it was a mistake to stay at home alone. She built a fire in the *fireplace* in the living room. The evening was not very cold, but she felt cold inside.

She heard the doorbell ring. "Who in the world –" Susan said to herself. It must be David, she thought. Of course! He had come to tell her about the ring. Mark would have found a way to get it back from David's grandmother.

To her surprise, Jeff and Betsy were at the door.

"Are you here alone?" Betsy asked.

"Yes. Come in," Susan said, stepping back from the door.

"We've got Griffin's car," Betsy said. "We're going to drive it out of town. Mark's going to follow us in Jeff's car. He's going to meet us here in a couple of minutes. We stopped to tell you that I've told my parents that I'm spending the night with you. Jeff told his parents that he's staying with Dave. Could you phone Dave and let him know?"

"Sure," Susan said and picked up the telephone. "David, it's Sue. Is everything all right?"

| *fireplace*, see picture, p. 57

"No," David said in a flat voice. "My grandmother died this morning."

"Oh, David! How awful!"

"It happened while my mother and I were at church. We found her lying on the floor in her bedroom. She must have fallen and hit her head when she was getting out of her chair."

"How terrible!" Susan said. "Is there anything I can do?"

"No," David said. "What did you call about?"

"Jeff and Betsy are here. They're on their way to get rid of the car. Jeff has told his parents he's spending the night at your house."

"He can't say that," David answered. "There are a lot of people from the church in the house with us right now."

"Well, Jeff will just have to change his story. David, the ring! Have you gotten it yet?"

"I don't want to think about that now. I'll look later, but not tonight. There's too much going on over here. The neighbor keeps saying that she saw someone in the bedroom with Grandma when she died. Someone wearing a brown sweater. My mother's very upset. Look, I've got to get back to my mother now. Good-bye."

"Good-bye." Susan hung up the phone. "His grandmother died today," she told Betsy and Jeff. "You can't tell your parents that you are staying at his house tonight, Jeff."

"Well, there's not much else I can do now," Jeff said. "Hey, what's the matter with you, Sue?"

"Mark has a brown sweater," Susan said suddenly. "He wears it all the time."

"What's that supposed to mean?"

"It means – it means –" Susan put her hand against the wall. "When I told Mark about the ring – he said – 'Don't worry. I'll get it.' There was someone with her when she died. The neighbor saw him."

5 "You're not making any sense," Betsy said. "What ring was Mark going to get?"

"Mr. Griffin's ring, the one that was missing from his finger when they found him. David took it."

"Dave did?" Jeff said in surprise. "My God, why?"

10 "Because – because –" She could not try to explain. It didn't matter any longer. "Mark killed that woman. He went over there this morning while David and his mother were in church, and he took the ring from her. He killed her!"

15 "You're crazy," Betsy said. "Mark would never do a thing like that."

"He would, and he did!" Suddenly, there was no doubt in her mind. "We've got to go to the police!"

"Betsy is right, you **are** crazy," Jeff said. "After all
20 we've gone through to keep this a secret, you want to go to the police **now**?"

"We have no choice anymore," Susan said.

"You don't have the right to make that decision," Betsy said. "We're all in this together. You agreed to
25 help with the kidnapping, and by doing that, you agreed to everything that followed."

"Didn't you hear a thing I said?" Susan asked her. "Mark killed Mrs. Ruggles! **He killed an old woman!** Mr. Griffin's death was an accident, but this wasn't.
30 Mark knew what he was doing. He planned it, and he killed her."

"You don't know that," Jeff said. "You don't have any proof."

74

"I don't need proof," Susan shouted. "The police can find that for me. If he killed her –"

"If he killed her, he did it to help us all, **you** as well," Betsy said. "He would have done it for us. If David was stupid enough to take that ring –" 5

"But he murdered her!" Susan said.

"You're only guessing that he did it, and you're probably wrong," Jeff said. "But if you're not, just remember that Mark did only what he had to do. He's gotten us through this until now, and he's going to get 10 us through this the rest of the way."

They heard a car outside.

"That's Mark," Betsy said. "What are we going to do?"

"It won't do us any good to get rid of the car if Sue is 15 going to the police," Jeff said. "We've got to keep her quiet."

"How?" Betsy asked.

"I'll stay with her. You run out and tell Mark what's happened. He'll think of something." 20

"You can't tell Mark!" Susan shouted. "He's the one who –"

But Jeff held her arms and Betsy was already out the door.

When she returned a few moments later, Mark was 25 with her. He was still wearing the brown sweater.

Chapter 18

"Where's her family?" Mark asked.

"Out for the evening," Jeff said. "There's nobody else here."

"Good. Betsy, find something to tie her up with."

"Betsy, no!" Susan shouted. "You can't keep doing everything he says, not when you know what he's done!"

"What exactly am I supposed to have done?" Mark asked.

"You killed Dave's grandmother," Susan said. "The neighbor saw you through the window."

"So maybe I was there. I went over to David's house and got the ring, like I told you I would. Why does that suddenly mean that I killed her? Old people fall down. It happens all the time."

Betsy came back into the room with a rope. Jeff held Susan's hands while Mark tied the rope around them.

What are they going to do to me? Susan thought, too scared to speak.

"And now what?" Jeff asked. "Are you thinking of leaving her in the mountains? I don't want to be a part of that."

"You're a part of whatever we do," Mark answered. "But, no, that's not the plan. People would guess she was there. We're staying with our plan. You and Betsy drive Griffin's car out of town, and I'll pick you up later in Jeff's car."

"But what about Sue?" Betsy asked. "We're just going to leave her here? What about when her parents come home? As soon as they're in the door, she'll tell them everything that happened."

"I don't think she'll do that," Mark said. "Don't worry. She won't tell the police."

"Jeff, please!" Susan said. "Don't leave me alone with him!"

"I want to know how you can be so sure that Susan won't talk to the police," Jeff said to Mark.

"I'm telling you for the last time, Jeff, I'll take care of things," Mark said angrily. "I've done all right until now, right? After you leave, Sue and I are just going to have a little talk. When we're done, she will have changed her mind about everything. Susan is just a little mixed up."

"You think you can *convince* her?" Jeff asked.

"Sure, he can," Betsy said. "He convinced her the last time, didn't he, when she and Dave found Mr. Griffin? If he could do it then, he can do it now."

"Stop worrying," Mark said. "Leave things to me, okay?"

"Okay," Jeff said.

"Let's go, Jeff," Betsy said and smiled at Susan. "You listen to Mark, Sue. Remember, he knows best."

"I – hate – you," Susan said. "I – hate – you – all."

"Well, we don't like you either," Betsy said with a laugh, and she and Jeff left.

When the door closed, Susan said to Mark, "You're not going to convince me of anything."

"I'm not even going to try," Mark answered coldly. "I'm just going to open the windows and let in a little air."

The wind blew in through the open window, causing the *flames* in the fireplace to grow.

"Watch out," Susan shouted. "You'll set the house on fire!"

"Setting fire to a house is not as easy as that," Mark said with a laugh. "It takes more work than that."

"What – what – do you mean?"

"You have to set fire to the curtains first. That's what

convince, make (someone) see things the way you see them
flame, see picture, p. 79

77

happened at our house. First the curtains and then –
whoosh! – the whole house!"

"I know," Susan said. "You told me. That's how your
father died, and I'm very sorry, Mark. Please let me go!"

5   "Don't be sorry," Mark said. "It was his own fault.
You know what he was going to do? He was going to
call the police because I had borrowed his credit card!"

"Mark, please untie me!"

"So you can go to the police? You must think I'm
10 pretty stupid. Why would I let you do that?"

"Because you have to," Susan said. "My parents will
be home in an hour or so, and I'll tell them. Oh, Mark,
go with me to the police – and say how awful it's been
– and how awful we feel. Can't we do that?"

15   "No," Mark said, holding a newspaper into the fire in
the fireplace. "We can't." Then he held the newspaper
to one of the curtains and set it on fire. "I never wanted
anything bad to happen to you, Sue," he said, looking
down at her, "but I never thought you would start acting
20 like this. When you're part of something, you can't just
stop being a part of it."

The flames ran up the curtain. Up, up, they went
until they reached the ceiling. Susan, lying on the floor
away from the windows, could feel the terrible heat
25 from the burning curtain.

I will be burned alive, Susan thought. "Mark!" she
tried to say, but no sound came out of her mouth.

"My father was going to tell the police," Mark said,
not looking at her anymore, "his only son – his only
30 child!"

He crossed the room and opened one of the other
windows. Just before she passed out, Susan saw two
people standing outside the window. One person

78

flame

caught Mark and pulled him out through the window. The other person was a woman who was staring at her.

I am going to die, Susan tried to say to the woman at the window. You're glad that this is happening to me, aren't you? What else can you be but glad?

Kathy Griffin looked straight at Susan, but there was no hate in her eyes. Her eyes looked sad. I would never want that to happen to you, her eyes said.

Chapter 19

Mrs. McConnell knocked on Susan's bedroom door and went in without waiting for an answer. She sat down on the edge of the bed.

"Sue," she said, "you can't go on like this. It's been ten days now, and it's time you began to get yourself together. We've got to talk about what happened."

"I don't want to talk about it," Susan said. "I don't even want to think about it."

"You have to. It's only by facing things that you ever put them behind you." Mrs. McConnell looked worried. "You never asked why Kathy Griffin and Detective Baca came to our house that night."

"Does it matter?" Susan asked.

"It certainly does. They saved your life. After reading the name Lana Turnboldt in the newspaper, Mrs. Griffin started thinking. She had heard the name before. When she read the name in the paper, she remembered that Lana was the girl who had given the English paper to Mark Kinney to copy. She worked out that he was the former boyfriend who also knew about the picnic place by the waterfall.

"She had met Mark at our house a few nights earlier, and he had been introduced as a friend of yours. She knew that you were the last person to have seen her husband. She started putting the pieces together and called Detective Baca. That's why they came to our house." *5*

"Okay, now I know," Susan said. "Do we have to keep talking about it?"

"Yes," her mother said, "we need to keep talking about it. Your father and I talked to a psychologist yesterday. *10* Detective Baca suggested it, and we found it very helpful. We need to understand what happened to you and the others who were under Mark's influence."

Susan looked at her mother. "What will happen to all of us?" *15*

"The police have said that Mark will be facing three *charges*: one for his part in Brian Griffin's death, one for the possible murder of Mrs. Ruggles, and one for what he tried to do to you. David, Betsy and Jeff will be charged with what happened in the mountains." *20*

"And me?"

"You weren't actually involved in what happened in the mountains," Mrs. McConnell said. "If you tell the police exactly what happened, you might be lucky."

"I don't think I can," Susan said. *25*

"You can, and you must," her mother said and took her hand. "You'll do whatever needs to be done. You've stayed in your room long enough now. Get dressed and come downstairs. I want you to come with me when I go shopping for new curtains." *30*

After her mother left the room, Susan sat on her bed

| *charge*, formal police statement that says you have committed a crime

for a long time. Then she got up and noticed a piece of paper lying on her desk:

"I found your homework among Brian's papers. He didn't have a chance to give it back to you. K. G."

5   Susan looked down at her English homework. How long ago it seemed that she had written it. At the bottom of the last page, Mr. Griffin had written:

Miss McConnell:

I was very happy to read your homework, which was excel-
10 *lent. I look forward to watching you grow as a writer and hope that I can continue helping you.*

                                            Brian Griffin

If she had been the Susan she was two weeks ago, she would have cried, but this new Susan had no more tears left to cry. She put the paper down on her desk
15 and started to get dressed.

Questions

Chapter 1

1. Why is Susan happy to walk to school together with David? What happens when they get to the school building?
2. What kind of teacher is Mr. Griffin? Do you think he is being fair to his students?
3. Which students don't hand in their English homework? Who does hand it in?

Chapter 2

1. What is Mark's plan? What do Jeff and Betsy think of it?
2. How does Mark convince them to join him? Why do they need David and Susan?
3. What happened when Jeff and Mark first met five years ago? What kind of person do you think Mark is?

Chapter 3

1. Who lives in David's house? Where is his father?
2. What is David's grandmother like?
3. Why do you think David agrees to join Mark?

Chapter 4

1. Who asks Susan to come to the picnic?
2. How does Mark know about the waterfall?
3. What does Susan say when she hears about Mark's plan?

Chapter 5

1. Why did Mr. Griffin want to teach high school students?
2. What does Mr. Griffin tell his wife he will do after school?
3. Why does he not tell Susan what a good student she is? What does Kathy tell him?

Chapter 6
1. What is David's surprise for his grandmother?
2. What is Betsy, Jeff and Mark's alibi?
3. What happens when they kidnap Mr. Griffin in the parking lot? Why does Susan cry?

Chapter 7
1. What happens to Betsy on her way to the mountains?
2. Does Mr. Griffin beg them to let him go?
3. When do they plan to come back to Mr. Griffin?

Chapter 8
1. Why is Susan so upset?
2. Why do Susan and David drive up into the mountains? Whose idea is it?
3. What do they find when they get to the waterfall?

Chapter 9
1. What does David suggest they do after they discover the body?
2. What reasons does Mark give for not reporting the death to the police?
3. What does Mark tell Susan happened to his father?

Chapter 10
1. What does David's grandmother remember about the Jell-O?
2. Why is it so important for David that his grandmother remembers the day before?
3. Who does Detective Baca want to talk to first? Why?

Chapter 11
1. Why does Susan go to school that morning?
2. How did Mark know that Susan would be called to the school office?

3. Why does Mark tell Susan to say she saw a woman together with Mr. Griffin?

Chapter 12
1. What does Mark do with Mr. Griffin's credit cards?
2. What does David do before they bury Mr. Griffin's body? Does it make any difference?
3. What happens at the airport parking lot? Why does the policeman remember Betsy?

Chapter 13
1. Who comes to the McConnells' house to talk to Susan?
2. Why does she think Susan is lying?
3. What part of Susan's story does she not believe? Why not?

Chapter 14
1. Who has found the plastic vial that Mr. Griffin's pills were in? Who is she?
2. Why is it a problem that Betsy was given a speeding ticket?
3. Why does Mark say that the news that the police have found Mr. Griffin's body is a trick?

Chapter 15
1. Why do you think David took the ring?
2. Who takes the ring from David? Why?
3. Who does Susan ask for help to get the ring back?

Chapter 16
1. What name is Kathy Griffin trying to remember?
2. How do you think Mr. Griffin died?
3. Who do you think has come to visit David's grandmother?

Chapter 17
1. What happened to David's grandmother? Who saw it happen?
2. How is killing David's grandmother different from killing Mr. Griffin?
3. How do Betsy and Jeff react when Susan tells them what she thinks Mark has done?

Chapter 18
1. How does Mark plan to make sure that Susan doesn't go to the police?
2. Has he ever done anything like this before?
3. Who does Susan see looking at her through the open window?

Chapter 19
1. Why were Detective Baca and Kathy Griffin at the McConnells' house?
2. Why does Susan's mother tell her that she needs to talk about what happened?
3. What did the note from Kathy Griffin say? How does Susan react when she has read Mr. Griffin's note? How do you think you would react?

Activities

1. Use as many of the following words as you can to write a short (2-3 pages) crime story of your own:

a.	scare	g.	bury
b.	threaten	h.	disappear
c.	beg	i.	steal
d.	blindfold	j.	lie
e.	pass out	k.	prove
f.	breathe	l.	convince

2. Many people in the story in this book tell lies to each other. Nine of the following ten statements are lies – and one of them is the truth. For each lie, write down who said it to whom, and why they said it. Which statement is true?

a. "Yesterday – Thursday – I came right home from school and gave you the Jell-O. Then we watched television all afternoon."

b. "I saw a woman in Mr. Griffin's car. I didn't see anything else or anyone else – just that."

c. "It tastes just fine. It's really good."

d. "There are lots of cars here. None of us wanted to miss this."

e. "I knew you'd join us, Sue! That's what I told the others."

f. "I don't remember her name anymore. Like I said, it was a bad time for me."

g. "There has to be a reason for Susan to have told the police all these lies."

h. "He and Mark are here in my room listening to music right now."

i. "Your mother went off to work this morning and forgot to make me lunch."

j. "After you leave, Sue and I are just going to have a little talk. When we're done, she will have changed her mind about everything."

3. In the story, Mark Kinney is very good at convincing his friends to do what he wants, no matter how serious the situation is. He uses many different kinds of arguments to convince them. Here are some of them:

a. "Look, if you are too scared, Jeff, just say so. There are plenty of others in that class who would help me. I can get all the help I want without you."

b. "Dave, how long has it been since you did something crazy? How long has it been since you did something wild, just for fun?"

c. "Betsy, your father is a County Commissioner. Just think what this would do to him. It would be in all the newspapers!"

d. "The point is, when it's your time to die, you die. You can't change anything. If we went to the police, it wouldn't bring Mr. Griffin back, would it? It wouldn't help at all. Nobody needs to know, Sue."

Find more ways that Mark Kinney uses to get people to do what he wants in the story. Would he convince you to join him?

In your class, form small groups of 4-5 students. In each group, one student pretends to be Mark Kinney, or someone like him, and one student pretends to be Susan McConnell, or someone like her. Then the student playing Mark should think of good ways of convincing the rest of the group to help him commit a crime. At the same time, the student playing Susan should think of good ways of convincing them **not** to help Mark. Get the other students to help you think of different kinds of arguments and write them down in a list. Would you use different arguments to convince different people? Are there arguments that would convince everyone? Which arguments do **you** think are the most convincing? Why? Compare your list with those of the other groups.

Find more exercises on
www.easyreader.dk